Be A Solution Provider

From Passion to Purpose

A Biblical Guide to
Being the Answer to the World!

Gerard Assey

Be A

Solution Provider

From Passion to Purpose

A Biblical Guide to

Being the Answer to the World!

By

Gerard Assey

Published by:

Gerard Assey

19/18, Palli Arasan Street

Anna Nagar East

Chennai - 600 102

ISBN: 978-81-965807-1-1

(Cover Image by jannoon028 on Freepik

www.freepik.com. Thank you)

Table of Contents

Preface

In a world filled with complexities and challenges, it's often easy to feel overwhelmed. We question our place in this vast, intricate web of existence and wonder if we can truly make a difference. Yet, deep within each of us lies a divine purpose, a calling to be a solution provider, a beacon of hope, and a force for positive change.

This book, **'Be A Solution Provider: *From Passion to Purpose- A Biblical Guide to Being the Answer to the World!'*** is a journey into the heart of that purpose. It's a reminder that you are here not by accident but by design, with a unique set of gifts and talents waiting to be unleashed for the betterment of humanity.

As we explore the profound lessons from the Scriptures and the timeless wisdom of those who walked before us, my hope is that you'll discover not only the calling that beckons you but also the courage and guidance to answer it. We'll delve into the art of empathy, the power of collaboration, the resilience to overcome obstacles, and the grace to navigate success with humility.

Through the lives of biblical figures and the teachings of sacred texts, we'll find inspiration and guidance. From Esther's courage to Gideon's faith, from the wisdom of King David to the generosity of Barnabas, their stories will illuminate our path.

In the pages that follow, we will finally explore how, through faith in Jesus Christ, we not only discover solutions but become walking answers to the world, for He is the Ultimate Solution, and His presence lives within us.

This book is not just a collection of words; it's an invitation to embark on a transformative journey—one that will empower you to leave a lasting legacy, one that will help you grow in your calling, and one that will remind you that, indeed, you are a solution provider to the world.

May you find solace and inspiration within these pages. May you uncover the brilliance of your purpose and embrace it with open arms. And may you, step into the world as a beacon of light and hope, ready to make a profound impact.

Importance of Viewing Yourself as a Solution Provider or an Answer to Someone's Problem in this World

Viewing yourself as a solution provider or as someone who can be the answer to someone's problem in this world is not only important from a practical standpoint but also aligns with several biblical principles and examples:

Biblical Examples

- ✓ **Fulfilling God's Plan:** The Bible teaches that each person is uniquely created with a purpose. When you view yourself as a solution provider, you are aligning with God's plan for your life. Just as God equipped individuals in the Bible for specific roles, recognizing your ability to solve problems and serve others can be a way of fulfilling your divine calling.
  Biblical Example: In the book of Exodus, Bezalel is mentioned as a man filled with the Spirit of God who had the skills and abilities to create beautiful craftsmanship for the Tabernacle. He used his talents to solve a problem by contributing to the construction of the Tabernacle, which played a vital role in the worship of God.
- ✓ **Reflecting Christ's Example:** Jesus Christ himself is the ultimate example of a solution provider. Throughout his ministry, he healed the sick, fed the hungry, comforted the brokenhearted, and offered salvation to all. By viewing yourself as a solution provider, you

are emulating the compassionate and transformative ministry of Christ.

Biblical Example: In the parable of the Good Samaritan, Jesus tells the story of a compassionate Samaritan who provides help to a wounded man on the road, demonstrating the concept of being a solution provider to those in need.

- ✓ **Exercising Stewardship:** The Bible teaches the principle of stewardship, where we are entrusted with resources and talents that are to be used for the greater good. Recognizing yourself as a solution provider acknowledges your responsibility to wisely steward the gifts and resources you've been given.

  Biblical Example: In the parable of the talents, Jesus tells the story of servants entrusted with varying amounts of money by their master. The servants who used their talents wisely and increased their master's wealth were praised. This parable illustrates the importance of using our gifts and resources effectively.

- ✓ **Living Out Love and Generosity:** The Bible emphasizes love for others and the importance of generosity. When you see yourself as a solution provider, you are actively living out these biblical principles by caring for the needs of others and demonstrating love through your actions.

  Biblical Example: Barnabas, often referred to as the "Son of Encouragement," sold his land and gave the proceeds to support the early Christian community. His generous act demonstrated a commitment to being a solution provider to the needs of others.

- ✓ **Leaving a Legacy of Impact:** The Bible contains numerous examples of individuals who left a lasting legacy through their acts of service and solution-providing. By viewing yourself in this way, you are positioning yourself to leave a meaningful legacy of positive impact.
  Biblical Example: Queen Esther risked her life to save her people from destruction. Her courage and willingness to address a critical problem left a legacy of deliverance for the Jewish people that is celebrated to this day during the feast of Purim.

Worldly Examples

- ✓ **Fulfilling Your Purpose:** Many believe that each individual has a unique purpose in life. Recognizing yourself as a solution provider aligns with the idea that you are here for a reason. By identifying and addressing problems, you fulfill your sense of purpose.
  Example: Mother Teresa dedicated her life to serving the impoverished and sick in Calcutta, India. By viewing herself as a solution provider to their suffering, she found profound purpose and made an immeasurable impact.
- ✓ **Positive Impact:** When you see yourself as a solution provider, you become a force for positive change. You actively seek ways to alleviate suffering, improve lives, and contribute to the betterment of society.
  Example: Dr. Jonas Salk, who developed the polio vaccine, saw himself as a solution

provider to the devastating polio epidemic. His work saved countless lives and is a testament to the impact of individuals who view themselves as answers to global health problems.

- ✓ **Empowerment:** This perspective empowers you. It instills a sense of agency and responsibility for the world's challenges. Instead of feeling overwhelmed, you become motivated to take action.
  Example: Malala Yousafzai, the Nobel laureate and education activist, viewed herself as a solution provider to the lack of educational opportunities for girls. Her unwavering determination led to educational reforms and advocacy for girls' education.
- ✓ **Building Relationships:** Being a solution provider fosters meaningful connections with others. People are drawn to those who offer help and support. It can strengthen personal and professional relationships.
  Example: Fred Rogers, the beloved TV host, viewed himself as a solution provider to children's emotional needs. His genuine care and commitment to children built strong, lasting connections with his audience.
- ✓ **Legacy:** Viewing yourself as a solution provider allows you to leave a lasting legacy. Your contributions to solving problems and making the world better will be remembered and continue to impact future generations.
  Example: Mahatma Gandhi saw himself as a solution provider to India's struggle for independence through nonviolent means. His

legacy of peaceful resistance and social change lives on today.

- ✓ **Personal Growth:** Embracing the role of a solution provider encourages personal growth. It challenges you to learn, adapt, and develop new skills to address complex issues.
  Example: Elon Musk, with his pursuit of sustainable energy solutions, constantly evolves and adapts his knowledge and skills to address global environmental challenges.

Viewing yourself as a solution provider is a mindset that empowers you to be a catalyst for positive change in the world. It enables you to recognize the potential within yourself to make a difference, no matter how big or small, and to leave a meaningful legacy that extends far beyond your lifetime.

In summary, viewing yourself as a solution provider aligns with biblical principles of purpose, stewardship, compassion, and love. It reflects the teachings and examples of Christ and empowers you to fulfill your unique calling in a way that honors God and benefits humanity.

Key Traits of Solution Providers

People who are solution providers or answers to the world's needs typically exhibit several key traits, both biblically and in the worldly context:

1. Compassion: Solution providers possess a deep sense of compassion for the suffering and needs of others. They are driven by a genuine desire to alleviate pain and improve lives.

Biblical Example: Jesus Christ, known for his compassion and healing of the sick, demonstrated the utmost compassion for humanity.

Worldly Example: Mother Teresa, whose unwavering compassion for the poor and sick in Calcutta led to the founding of the Missionaries of Charity and a lifetime of service.

2. Empathy: They have the ability to empathize with the struggles and challenges faced by others. This empathy allows them to connect on a profound level and truly understand the needs of those they aim to help.

Biblical Example: The parable of the Good Samaritan highlights empathy in action as the Samaritan cares for a wounded man he encounters on the road.

Worldly Example: Oprah Winfrey, who uses her platform to address various societal issues with empathy, understanding, and compassion.

3. Humility: Solution providers approach their role with humility, recognizing that their actions are in service to a greater cause. They are not motivated by personal recognition but by the desire to make a difference.

Biblical Example: King David, despite his accomplishments, remained humble before God, as demonstrated in his Psalms and actions.
Worldly Example: Mahatma Gandhi, who led India to independence through nonviolent resistance, embodied humility in his leadership.
4. **Resilience:** They demonstrate resilience in the face of obstacles and setbacks. Challenges do not deter them; instead, they view them as opportunities for growth and learning.
Biblical Example: The prophet Jeremiah faced immense opposition and persecution but remained resilient in his commitment to God's calling.
Worldly Example: Thomas Edison, who famously said, "I have not failed. I've just found 10,000 ways that won't work," exemplified resilience in his pursuit of inventing the light bulb.
5. **Integrity:** Solution providers uphold high standards of honesty and integrity in their actions. They are trustworthy and maintain ethical conduct.
Biblical Example: The integrity of Daniel, who refused to compromise his faith and values even in the face of adversity, is evident in the Bible.
Worldly Example: Abraham Lincoln, known for his unwavering commitment to moral principles during his presidency, exemplified integrity.
6. **Vision:** They have a clear vision of the problems they aim to solve and the impact they want to make. This vision guides their actions and decisions.
Biblical Example: Nehemiah, who had a clear vision to rebuild the walls of Jerusalem, led a successful reconstruction project.
Worldly Example: Steve Jobs, who had a vision of bringing innovative technology to the masses, co-

founded Apple Inc. and revolutionized the tech industry.

7. Generosity: Solution providers often exhibit a spirit of generosity, willingly giving of their time, resources, and expertise to benefit others.

Biblical Example: Barnabas, who sold his land to support the early Christian community, demonstrated generosity.

Worldly Example: Bill and Melinda Gates, through their philanthropic foundation, have donated billions to address global health and poverty issues.

8. Perseverance: They display perseverance and determination, especially when faced with long-term or complex problems. They do not easily give up but stay committed to their mission.

Biblical Example: Nehemiah's determination to rebuild Jerusalem's walls in the face of opposition and challenges illustrates perseverance.

Worldly Example: Nelson Mandela, who spent 27 years in prison for his anti-apartheid activism, persevered and later became South Africa's first black president.

These key traits, whether seen in biblical figures or in contemporary individuals, define solution providers and those who are answers to the world's needs. They serve as role models for making a positive impact and leaving a lasting legacy in the world.

Making a Meaningful Difference in this World

In the grand tapestry of life, each one of us is woven with a unique thread, carefully placed by the Creator's hand. We all share a profound purpose, a calling if you will, to make a meaningful difference in this world. It is a purpose rooted in the essence of our existence, a purpose that transcends the ordinary, and a purpose that often revolves around being a solution provider to those around us.

Lesson 1: Recognizing Your Unique Gifts Embedded within each of us are talents and abilities that set us apart. The Bible reminds us of this truth in 1 Corinthians 12:4-6, "Now there are varieties of gifts, but the same Spirit; and there are varieties of service, but the same Lord; and there are varieties of activities, but it is the same God who empowers them all in everyone."

Action Plan: Take a moment for self-reflection. Identify your unique gifts and talents. What are you exceptionally good at? How can you employ these abilities to provide solutions to the challenges you encounter?

Strategy: Focus on honing your gifts through continuous learning and practice. Be prepared to leverage these gifts for the betterment of others.

Lesson 2: Developing a Heart for Others Compassion and empathy lie at the heart of every solution provider's journey. Colossians 3:12-13 guides us in this aspect, "Put on then, as God's chosen ones, holy and beloved, compassionate hearts, kindness, humility, meekness, and patience, bearing with one another and, if one has a complaint against another, forgiving each other; as the Lord has forgiven you, so you also must forgive."

Action Plan: Cultivate a heart of compassion. Make a conscious effort to understand the challenges faced by others and show kindness and patience.

Strategy: Listen actively to the needs and concerns of those around you. Offer your support and help where you can.

Lesson 3: Seeking Divine Guidance In the pursuit of providing solutions, seeking divine wisdom is paramount. James 1:5 reassures us, "If any of you lacks wisdom, let him ask God, who gives generously to all without reproach, and it will be given him."

Action Plan: Dedicate time for prayer and reflection. Seek God's guidance when faced with challenging decisions or problems.

Strategy: Develop a habit of seeking divine wisdom in your daily life. Trust that God will equip you with the insights needed to address the issues that come your way.

Lesson 4: Honesty and Integrity Building trust and credibility is essential in the journey of a solution provider. Proverbs 11:3 reminds us, "The integrity of the upright guides them, but the crookedness of the treacherous destroys them."

Action Plan: Commit to living a life of honesty and integrity. Be truthful in all your dealings.

Strategy: Uphold your reputation by consistently demonstrating integrity. This will not only build trust but also open doors for greater opportunities to provide solutions.

Lesson 5: Persistence and Resilience Obstacles are an inevitable part of the journey. Philippians 4:13 encourages us, "I can do all things through him who strengthens me."

Action Plan: Develop resilience by embracing challenges as opportunities for growth.
Strategy: Stay committed to your purpose, even when faced with adversity. Draw strength from your faith and your belief in your ability to overcome obstacles.

As we embark on this journey of becoming solution providers, let us remember that our purpose is divinely ordained. Through these lessons and strategies, we will explore how to fulfill this purpose and leave a lasting impact on the world.

Understanding Your Calling

Each of us is crafted with a unique set of talents and gifts, specially bestowed upon us by the Divine Creator. These gifts are not random; they are purposefully designed to fulfill a greater plan. In this chapter, we embark on a journey to recognize these special endowments and understand how they tie into our divine calling as solution providers.

Lesson: Recognizing Your Unique Gifts Every individual possesses a set of talents that distinguish them from others. These gifts are not limited to grandiose abilities but can encompass simple, yet profound skills that can be used to make a difference. As the Apostle Paul writes in 1 Corinthians 12:4-6, "Now there are varieties of gifts, but the same Spirit; and there are varieties of service, but the same Lord; and there are varieties of activities, but it is the same God who empowers them all in everyone."

Biblical Example: Bezalel - The Craftsman One inspiring biblical example of someone who recognized and effectively used his unique gifts is Bezalel. He was chosen by God to be the chief artisan for the construction of the Tabernacle. Bezalel possessed exceptional craftsmanship and artistic skills, and he employed these talents to create the sacred furnishings and structures as described in Exodus 31:1-5. His work not only served a practical purpose but also played a significant role in the spiritual life of the community.

Action Plan: Self-Assessment of Gifts and Talents To begin your journey as a solution provider, it's essential to conduct an honest and introspective self-assessment. Take time to reflect on your skills, talents, and interests. What are you naturally good at? What activities bring you joy and satisfaction? Consider seeking input from trusted friends and mentors who can provide valuable insights into your strengths.

Strategy: Leveraging Your Gifts for Impact Once you've identified your unique gifts, the next step is to discern how they can be leveraged to make a positive impact on the world. This may involve aligning your talents with specific needs or problems you encounter in your community, workplace, or personal life. Remember that the purpose of your gifts is not for self-aggrandizement but to serve others and contribute to a greater good.

Prompts for Journaling and Self-Reflection

Use the following prompts as a guide for your journaling and self-reflection. Writing down your thoughts and experiences can provide clarity, deepen your understanding, and inspire continued growth as a solution provider.

Recognizing Your Unique Gifts: Reflect on the talents and gifts you've been blessed with. How can you use these gifts to solve problems and make a positive impact in the world?

Practical Exercises and Reflection Questions to Help You Apply the Concepts

Exercise:

- ✓ Take a personal inventory of your unique gifts and talents. List at least three gifts or skills you possess that you believe can be used to solve problems or make a positive impact in the world.

Reflection Questions:

- ✓ How do your unique gifts align with your sense of purpose?
- ✓ Can you think of a specific problem or challenge where you could apply these gifts to make a difference?

Action Plan with Strategies to Help You Take Forward and Implement

Action Plan: Begin by conducting a self-assessment of your gifts and talents. Make a list of your strengths, skills, and areas where you excel. Seek feedback from friends and mentors to gain a comprehensive understanding of your unique gifts.

Strategy: Once you've identified your gifts, consider how they can be applied to solve specific problems or serve a particular need. For example, if you have a talent for storytelling, you can use this skill to create content that inspires and educates others.

As you delve into this chapter, reflect on the lessons of recognizing your unique gifts, take inspiration from the biblical example of Bezalel, conduct a thorough self-assessment, and consider strategies for leveraging your gifts effectively. This is the foundation upon which you will build your journey as a solution provider, making a meaningful difference in the lives of those you touch.

Compassion and Empathy

In our journey to become solution providers, we come to a crossroad where compassion and empathy serve as guiding lights. These qualities, deeply rooted in the human heart, are vital in our quest to make a positive impact on the lives of others. In this chapter, we explore the profound significance of compassion and empathy, drawing wisdom from the Scriptures and the actions of those who exemplified these virtues.

Lesson: Developing a Heart for Others Compassion and empathy are the cornerstones of our mission as solution providers. In Colossians 3:12-13, the Apostle Paul implores us, "Put on then, as God's chosen ones, holy and beloved, compassionate hearts, kindness, humility, meekness, and patience, bearing with one another and, if one has a complaint against another, forgiving each other; as the Lord has forgiven you, so you also must forgive."

Biblical Example: The Good Samaritan A timeless illustration of compassion and empathy is found in the parable of the Good Samaritan, as recounted in Luke 10:25-37. Here, a Samaritan traveler demonstrates compassion by caring for a wounded stranger, despite their cultural differences and social barriers. This act of selflessness serves as a powerful reminder that compassion knows no boundaries.

Action Plan: Practicing Empathy To develop a heart for others, we must actively practice empathy in our daily lives. This begins with intentionally placing ourselves in the shoes of those we encounter. Empathy is about genuinely understanding and sharing the feelings of others, whether they are experiencing joy or sorrow.

Strategy: Listening and Understanding Needs A core component of empathy is the art of listening attentively. Make it a point to engage in deep, empathetic listening when interacting with people. Take time to understand their needs, fears, and aspirations. By doing so, you not only demonstrate your compassion but also gain valuable insights into how you can provide meaningful solutions.

Prompts for Journaling and Self-Reflection
Use the following prompts as a guide for your journaling and self-reflection. Writing down your thoughts and experiences can provide clarity, deepen your understanding, and inspire continued growth as a solution provider.
Moments of Compassion: Describe a recent experience where you showed compassion and empathy towards someone. How did it make you feel, and what impact did it have on the other person?

Practical Exercises and Reflection Questions to Help You Apply the Concepts
Exercise:

- ✓ Practice active listening in a conversation with a friend or family member. Focus on genuinely understanding their perspective without offering immediate solutions.

Reflection Questions:

- ✓ What did you learn from actively listening to the other person?
- ✓ How can you incorporate empathy into your daily interactions to better understand the needs of others?

Action Plan with Strategies to Help You Take Forward and Implement

Action Plan: Dedicate time each week to engage in acts of kindness and empathy. This could be as simple as volunteering at a local charity, helping a neighbor in need, or actively listening to a friend going through a difficult time.

Strategy: Make a conscious effort to practice active listening in your interactions with others. When someone shares their problems or concerns, empathize with their emotions and offer support. For instance, if a colleague is stressed at work, take the time to listen and provide encouragement.

As you delve into this chapter, consider the lesson of developing a heart for others, drawing inspiration from the parable of the Good Samaritan. Begin to practice empathy in your daily interactions, and prioritize the art of listening and understanding the needs of those around you. Compassion and empathy are not only essential qualities in your journey as a solution provider but also powerful catalysts for positive change in the world.

Problem-Solving with Wisdom

As solution providers, we encounter a myriad of challenges and obstacles along our journey. In these moments, seeking divine guidance and harnessing the power of wisdom becomes paramount. This chapter delves into the profound significance of wisdom, as we explore how it is cultivated through faith, as exemplified in the Scriptures and the life of Solomon.

Lesson: Seeking Divine Guidance In the complex tapestry of life's challenges, seeking divine guidance is akin to navigating with a compass. James 1:5 reminds us, "If any of you lacks wisdom, let him ask God, who gives generously to all without reproach, and it will be given him."

Biblical Example: Solomon's Wisdom Solomon, renowned for his wisdom, stands as an exemplary figure in the Bible. In 1 Kings 3:5-14, Solomon's request for wisdom to govern God's people serves as a testament to the profound impact of seeking divine guidance. God granted his request, and Solomon's wisdom was instrumental in resolving intricate disputes and dilemmas.

Action Plan: Prayer and Seeking Wisdom To access divine wisdom, cultivate a habit of earnest prayer and seeking God's guidance. Dedicate time each day for reflection and communion with the Divine. Approach God with an open heart, ready to receive the wisdom needed to navigate life's complexities.

Strategy: Making Informed Decisions Wisdom is not merely the accumulation of knowledge but the ability to make informed and discerning decisions. As you encounter challenges and problems, draw upon the wisdom acquired through prayer and reflection. Evaluate your options carefully, consider the consequences, and seek counsel from trusted individuals who can provide valuable insights.

Prompts for Journaling and Self-Reflection

Use the following prompts as a guide for your journaling and self-reflection. Writing down your thoughts and experiences can provide clarity, deepen your understanding, and inspire continued growth as a solution provider.

Seeking Divine Guidance: Share a situation in your life where you sought divine guidance or wisdom. How did this guidance influence your decisions and actions?

Practical Exercises and Reflection Questions to Help You Apply the Concepts

Exercise:

- ✓ Before making a significant decision, spend time in prayer or meditation seeking guidance. Reflect on any insights or feelings that arise during this process.

Reflection Questions:

- ✓ How did seeking divine guidance influence your decision-making process?
- ✓ What strategies can you develop to make more informed and wisdom-guided decisions?

Action Plan with Strategies to Help You Take Forward and Implement

Action Plan: Establish a daily routine of prayer and meditation to seek divine guidance in your decision-making. Create a journal to record your thoughts and insights that arise during these moments of reflection.
Strategy: Before making significant decisions, consult with trusted mentors or spiritual advisors. Share your dilemmas and seek their counsel. For example, if you're facing a career decision, meet with a mentor who can provide guidance rooted in their own experiences.

In this chapter, reflect upon the lesson of seeking divine guidance, drawing inspiration from James 1:5, and the wisdom of Solomon. Embrace a habit of prayer and the pursuit of wisdom. Recognize that wisdom is not a static attribute but a dynamic force that empowers you to make informed decisions, ultimately enhancing your role as a solution provider.

Building Trust and Credibility

In our journey as solution providers, trust and credibility are the bedrock upon which our impact is built. These qualities are not earned overnight; they are cultivated through a steadfast commitment to honesty and integrity. In this chapter, we explore the profound significance of trustworthiness, drawing wisdom from the Scriptures and the unwavering integrity of biblical figures like Daniel.

Lesson: Honesty and Integrity Honesty and integrity form the foundation of trust. As Proverbs 11:3 tells us, "The integrity of the upright guides them, but the crookedness of the treacherous destroys them." It's a reminder that a life built on honesty and integrity is like a sturdy pillar that withstands the test of time.

Biblical Example: Daniel's Integrity Daniel's unwavering commitment to integrity is showcased throughout the Book of Daniel. His refusal to compromise his faith or principles, even when faced with dire consequences, sets an inspiring example. His integrity led to favor, trust, and influence in the Babylonian court, as seen in Daniel 6:3-5.

Action Plan: Living a Life of Integrity To build trust and credibility, we must make integrity an integral part of our character. Start by examining your own actions and choices. Are they aligned with your values? Commit to being truthful, consistent, and honest in all your dealings, whether personal or professional.

Strategy: Establishing Trustworthy Relationships
Building trust extends beyond personal integrity. It also involves establishing and nurturing trustworthy relationships. Be reliable and dependable in your commitments to others. Fulfill promises and obligations consistently. Over time, this reliability will foster trust in your relationships.

Prompts for Journaling and Self-Reflection
Use the following prompts as a guide for your journaling and self-reflection. Writing down your thoughts and experiences can provide clarity, deepen your understanding, and inspire continued growth as a solution provider.
Building Trust and Credibility: Consider instances in which you've faced ethical dilemmas. How did you uphold honesty and integrity in those situations, and what were the outcomes?

Practical Exercises and Reflection Questions to Help you Apply the Concepts
Exercise:

- ✓ Identify a situation where you had to make an ethical decision. Reflect on how you upheld honesty and integrity, and what impact it had on your relationships.

Reflection Questions:

- ✓ How did your commitment to honesty and integrity affect the outcome of the situation?
- ✓ What steps can you take to ensure you maintain trust and credibility in future situations?

Action Plan with Strategies to Help You Take Forward and Implement

Action Plan: Develop a personal code of ethics and principles that reflect your commitment to honesty and integrity. Review and refine this code regularly to ensure it aligns with your values.
Strategy: When faced with ethical challenges, be transparent about your decision-making process. For instance, if you encounter a situation at work where honesty is crucial, communicate openly with your colleagues about the ethical considerations involved.

As you delve into this chapter, reflect upon the lesson of honesty and integrity, drawing wisdom from Proverbs 11:3, and the life of Daniel as a shining example. Embrace a life characterized by unwavering integrity and establish trustworthy relationships built on reliability and consistency. In doing so, you will fortify the trust and credibility essential for your role as a solution provider.

Persistence and Resilience

In the pursuit of our calling as solution providers, we inevitably encounter obstacles and challenges that test our resolve. It's during these trying moments that the qualities of persistence and resilience come to the forefront, allowing us to overcome adversity and continue our mission. In this chapter, we explore the profound significance of resilience and the strength it provides, drawing wisdom from the Scriptures and the inspirational story of Nehemiah rebuilding the wall of Jerusalem.

Lesson: Overcoming Obstacles: Obstacles are not roadblocks but stepping stones on the path to growth and transformation. The lesson of overcoming obstacles is beautifully encapsulated in Philippians 4:13, which reassures us, "I can do all things through him who strengthens me."

Biblical Example: Nehemiah Rebuilding the Wall The biblical account of Nehemiah is a testament to the power of resilience. Nehemiah faced the seemingly insurmountable task of rebuilding the walls of Jerusalem, a project plagued with opposition and adversity. Despite the challenges, he displayed unwavering determination, as seen in Nehemiah 4:6, "So we built the wall, for the people had a mind to work."

Action Plan: Developing Perseverance To develop resilience, it's crucial to cultivate perseverance as a personal attribute. Embrace challenges as opportunities for growth rather than setbacks. When faced with adversity, don't be discouraged; instead, view it as a chance to learn, adapt, and improve.

Strategy: Staying Committed in the Face of Challenges Resilience is not a one-time feat but a continuous commitment to staying the course, even in the face of seemingly insurmountable challenges. Stay focused on your goals and vision. Surround yourself with a support network of individuals who can offer encouragement and guidance during tough times.

Prompts for Journaling and Self-Reflection

Use the following prompts as a guide for your journaling and self-reflection. Writing down your thoughts and experiences can provide clarity, deepen your understanding, and inspire continued growth as a solution provider.

Your Role as a Solution Provider: What does being a solution provider mean to you on a personal level? How do you envision your journey evolving as you continue to grow in this role?

Practical Exercises and Reflection Questions to Help You Apply the Concepts

Exercise:

- ✓ Choose a personal goal or project you've been hesitant to pursue due to obstacles. Develop a plan to overcome one specific obstacle and take the first step.

Reflection Questions:

- ✓ What challenges did you encounter when taking action to overcome the obstacle?
- ✓ How can you stay committed to your goals in the face of adversity?

Action Plan with Strategies to Help You Take Forward and Implement

Action Plan: Embrace challenges as opportunities for growth. Create a "resilience toolbox" filled with strategies that help you cope with adversity, such as mindfulness exercises, stress management techniques, or inspirational quotes.

Strategy: Learn from the examples of resilient individuals, like Nelson Mandela, who persevered through years of imprisonment. Study their stories and draw inspiration from their ability to overcome seemingly insurmountable obstacles.

As you immerse yourself in this chapter, reflect on the lesson of overcoming obstacles, drawing wisdom from Philippians 4:13 and the inspiring example of Nehemiah. Develop the virtue of perseverance and commit to staying the course, no matter how challenging it may become. Through persistence and resilience, you'll find the strength to continue your journey as a solution provider, undeterred by adversity.

The Power of Collaboration

In this journey as solution providers, we often find that the most significant impact is achieved when we come together with others, working collaboratively towards a shared purpose. This chapter delves into the profound significance of collaboration, emphasizing the lessons we can glean from the Scriptures, particularly from Ecclesiastes 4:9-12, and the harmonious ministry of the apostles.

Lesson: Working Together for a Common Goal Collaboration is more than just cooperation; it is the art of working together harmoniously, synergizing efforts, and combining strengths to achieve a common goal. Ecclesiastes 4:9-12 beautifully captures this lesson: "Two are better than one, because they have a good reward for their toil. For if they fall, one will lift up his fellow. But woe to him who is alone when he falls and has not another to lift him up!"

Biblical Example: The Apostles' Ministry The early Christian community, particularly the ministry of the apostles, is a remarkable biblical example of effective collaboration. These individuals came together, each contributing their unique gifts and strengths, to spread the message of faith, hope, and love. They complemented one another's abilities and played vital roles in building the foundation of the Christian faith.

Action Plan: Building a Support Network To harness the power of collaboration, start by building a support network. Identify individuals who share your vision and values. Seek out those whose strengths complement your own. Cultivate relationships founded on trust, respect, and a shared commitment to your common purpose.

Strategy: Leveraging Collective Strength Effective collaboration involves not just the pooling of resources but also the collective strength of diverse perspectives and skills. Encourage open communication within your collaborative team, valuing each member's input. Be willing to adapt and make decisions that benefit the greater good.

Prompts for Journaling and Self-Reflection
Use the following prompts as a guide for your journaling and self-reflection. Writing down your thoughts and experiences can provide clarity, deepen your understanding, and inspire continued growth as a solution provider.
Collaborative Moments: Reflect on successful collaborations you've been a part of. What made these collaborations effective, and how did they contribute to your mission as a solution provider?

Practical Exercises and Reflection Questions to Help You Apply the Concepts
Exercise:

- ✓ Identify a cause or project you're passionate about and seek out potential collaborators who share your vision. Initiate a conversation or partnership with them.

Reflection Questions:

- ✓ How did the collaborative process enhance your ability to address the chosen cause or project?
- ✓ What lessons did you learn about working together for a common goal?

Action Plan with Strategies to Help You Take Forward and Implement

Action Plan: Identify potential collaborators who share your mission and values. Reach out to them and initiate conversations about potential partnerships or projects.

Strategy: Look to historical examples of successful collaborations, such as the partnership between Steve Jobs and Steve Wozniak in founding Apple Inc. Study how their complementary skills and shared vision propelled them to success.

As you immerse yourself in this chapter, reflect on the lesson of working together for a common goal, drawing wisdom from Ecclesiastes 4:9-12, and the collaborative efforts of the apostles. Take action to build a support network of like-minded individuals and learn to leverage the collective strength of your team. In doing so, you'll discover the transformative power of collaboration in your mission as a solution provider.

Giving Back and Generosity

As we move along in this pursuit of being solution providers, we come to realize that one of the most profound ways to make an enduring impact is through the spirit of giving back and practicing generosity. This chapter explores the transformative power of generosity, drawing inspiration from the teachings of Luke 6:38 and the exemplary life of Barnabas, the encourager.

Lesson: Sharing Your Blessings Generosity is born out of the heart's willingness to share the blessings one has received. In Luke 6:38, Jesus imparts this timeless wisdom: "Give, and it will be given to you. A good measure, pressed down, shaken together and running over, will be poured into your lap. For with the measure you use, it will be measured to you."

Biblical Example: Barnabas the Encourager Barnabas, whose name means "son of encouragement," is a biblical exemplar of generosity. In Acts 4:36-37, he sold a field and brought the proceeds to the apostles to support the early Christian community. His generous spirit went beyond material possessions; he also encouraged and mentored others, such as the young Saul who would later become the Apostle Paul.

Action Plan: Cultivating a Generous Spirit To cultivate a generous spirit, start by recognizing the abundance in your life. Reflect on the blessings, talents, and resources you've been granted. Begin by acknowledging that generosity is not solely about material giving but extends to giving your time, compassion, and support.

Strategy: Impacting Lives through Generosity: Generosity is a transformative force that can profoundly impact the lives of others. Create a plan for giving back, whether through financial contributions to causes you believe in, volunteering your time, or offering your expertise to those in need. Remember that generosity is not only about the immediate impact but also about planting seeds of positive change that can flourish over time.

Prompts for Journaling and Self-Reflection

Use the following prompts as a guide for your journaling and self-reflection. Writing down your thoughts and experiences can provide clarity, deepen your understanding, and inspire continued growth as a solution provider.

Generosity in Action: Share an experience where you practiced generosity. How did it impact your perspective on giving, and what positive change did it bring about?

Practical Exercises and Reflection Questions to Help You Apply the Concepts

Exercise:

- ✓ Dedicate a specific amount of time or resources to a charitable or community service activity. Document your experiences and emotions during this act of generosity.

Reflection Questions:

- ✓ How did the act of giving back impact your perspective on generosity?

- ✓ How can you continue to incorporate generosity into your life on an ongoing basis?

Action Plan with Strategies to Help You Take Forward and Implement

Action Plan: Establish a giving budget as part of your financial planning. Allocate a percentage of your income to charitable donations or causes that align with your values.

Strategy: Research philanthropic initiatives that resonate with you, such as Bill and Melinda Gates' efforts to combat global health issues. Learn from their strategic approach to giving and the impact it has had.

As you immerse yourself in this chapter, reflect on the lesson of sharing your blessings, drawing wisdom from Luke 6:38, and the life of Barnabas as an embodiment of generosity. Take concrete steps to cultivate a generous spirit within yourself and devise strategies to impact lives through your acts of kindness and giving. In doing so, you'll discover the immeasurable joy and fulfillment that comes from giving back to others.

Leaving a Legacy

Moving forward as solution providers, we are driven not only by the desire to solve immediate problems but also by the aspiration to leave a lasting impact that extends beyond our own lifetime. This chapter explores the profound notion of legacy, drawing inspiration from the teachings of Matthew 5:16 and the courageous life of Esther.

Lesson: Making a Lasting Impact Legacy is about making a mark that endures, transcending the boundaries of time. As Matthew 5:16 reminds us, "Let your light shine before others, so that they may see your good works and give glory to your Father who is in heaven." It underscores the idea that our actions and contributions can illuminate the path for others.

Biblical Example: Esther's Courage Esther's story is a compelling illustration of making a lasting impact. Faced with a life-altering decision, she summoned the courage to approach the Persian king and advocate for her people. Her bravery and selflessness not only saved her people from impending doom but also set an example of extraordinary courage and faith.

Action Plan: Defining Your Legacy To leave a meaningful legacy, it's essential to define what you wish to be remembered for. Reflect on your values, passions, and the impact you aspire to make. What positive changes do you hope to bring about in your community, family, or profession?

Strategy: Creating a Positive Impact on Future Generations A lasting legacy often involves planting seeds of positive change that can grow and flourish for generations to come. Consider how your actions, choices, and contributions can shape the future. Mentor and inspire the next generation, instilling in them the values and principles you hold dear.

Prompts for Journaling and Self-Reflection

Use the following prompts as a guide for your journaling and self-reflection. Writing down your thoughts and experiences can provide clarity, deepen your understanding, and inspire continued growth as a solution provider.

Defining Your Legacy: Imagine yourself looking back on your life many years from now. What legacy do you hope to leave behind? What steps can you take today to work toward that legacy?

Practical Exercises and Reflection Questions to Help You Apply the Concepts

Exercise:

- ✓ Begin drafting a personal mission statement that outlines the impact you hope to leave on the world. Continuously refine this statement as you reflect on your journey.

Reflection Questions:

- ✓ What elements are essential to your personal mission statement?
- ✓ How can you align your daily actions with the legacy you aspire to leave?

Action Plan with Strategies to Help You Take Forward and Implement

Action Plan: Begin drafting a personal mission statement that encapsulates the impact you wish to make in your lifetime. Continuously refine and adapt this statement as your journey evolves.
Strategy: Explore the legacies of inspirational figures like Mahatma Gandhi, whose commitment to nonviolence and social justice continues to inspire generations. Analyze their methods for creating enduring change.

As you delve into this chapter, reflect on the lesson of making a lasting impact, drawing wisdom from Matthew 5:16, and the courageous example of Esther. Take deliberate steps to define your legacy, envisioning the positive impact you wish to create in the world. Develop strategies that focus on nurturing and inspiring future generations, ensuring that your legacy is one of enduring significance and positive change.

Balancing Success and Humility

In the pursuit of our calling as solution providers, we often encounter success and achievement on our path. While these moments can be exhilarating, they also present us with a profound challenge—to remain grounded in humility. This chapter explores the delicate balance between success and humility, drawing inspiration from the teachings of Proverbs 27:2 and the life of the biblical figure King David.

Lesson: Remaining Grounded in Success: Success can be a double-edged sword; while it brings recognition and accomplishment, it can also sow the seeds of pride and arrogance. Proverbs 27:2 wisely cautions us: "Let another praise you, and not your own mouth; a stranger, and not your own lips." It reminds us of the virtue of humility in the face of success.

Biblical Example: King David's Humility King David, known for his victories in battle and his role in establishing the kingdom of Israel, also exemplified remarkable humility. Even in the height of his success, he recognized his dependence on God and acknowledged his shortcomings. His humility is evident in Psalms such as Psalm 51, where he repents and seeks God's mercy.

Action Plan: Cultivating Humility To cultivate humility in the face of success, begin by acknowledging that your achievements are not solely the result of your efforts. Recognize the contributions of others, the role of providence, and the support you've received along the way. Practice gratitude for the opportunities that success has bestowed upon you.

Strategy: Staying Humble Amidst Achievements
Humility is a continuous journey, not a destination. Stay connected with your values and principles, even as you achieve success. Seek accountability through trusted friends and mentors who can provide honest feedback and keep you grounded. Regularly engage in self-reflection to evaluate your actions and motivations.

Prompts for Journaling and Self-Reflection
Use the following prompts as a guide for your journaling and self-reflection. Writing down your thoughts and experiences can provide clarity, deepen your understanding, and inspire continued growth as a solution provider.
Balancing Success and Humility: Reflect on a moment of personal success. How did you maintain humility in the face of achievement, and what lessons did you learn from this balance?

Practical Exercises and Reflection Questions to Help You Apply the Concepts
Exercise:

- ✓ Create a gratitude journal to record daily moments of success, no matter how small. Reflect on the role of humility in your achievements.

Reflection Questions:

- ✓ How does practicing gratitude impact your perception of success and humility?

- ✓ How can you ensure you remain grounded in humility as you achieve your goals?

Action Plan with Strategies to Help You Take Forward and Implement

Action Plan: Practice daily gratitude by keeping a gratitude journal. Reflect on your achievements, recognizing the role of others and providence in your success.

Strategy: Study the lives of humble leaders like Mother Teresa, who dedicated her life to serving the impoverished. Understand how their humility fueled their impact on the world.

As you delve into this chapter, reflect on the lesson of remaining grounded in success, drawing wisdom from Proverbs 27:2, and the humble example of King David. Develop an action plan that focuses on cultivating humility in your daily life and strategies for staying humble amidst achievements. By doing so, you'll not only achieve success but also exemplify the enduring virtue of humility, making your journey as a solution provider all the more impactful and meaningful.

Overcoming Doubt and Fear

In our exploration as solution providers, there will be moments when doubt and fear threaten to paralyze our progress. These inner struggles can be formidable obstacles, but they are also opportunities for growth and unwavering faith. This chapter delves into the profound lesson of overcoming doubt and fear, drawing inspiration from the comforting words of Jeremiah 29:11 and the unwavering faith of Gideon.

Lesson: Trusting in God's Plan Amidst doubt and fear, it is essential to trust in God's plan for our lives. Jeremiah 29:11 assures us of this truth: "For I know the plans I have for you, declares the Lord, plans for welfare and not for evil, to give you a future and a hope." This verse reminds us that God's purpose for us is rooted in love, hope, and a promising future.

Biblical Example: Gideon's Faith Gideon's story in the book of Judges is a testament to unwavering faith in the face of doubt and fear. When called by God to lead the Israelites against their oppressors, Gideon questioned his abilities and sought multiple signs from God for confirmation. Despite his initial doubt and fear, Gideon eventually stepped into his role as a leader with remarkable faith and achieved victory through God's guidance.

Action Plan: Conquering Fear and Doubt To conquer fear and doubt, start by acknowledging these emotions rather than suppressing them. Understand that they are natural human responses. Turn to prayer and meditation to find solace and clarity. Seek the support of trusted friends and mentors who can provide guidance and encouragement during moments of uncertainty.

Strategy: Embracing God's Purpose for You
Embracing God's purpose for your life is a journey of surrender and faith. Reflect on your unique calling and talents, and consider how they can be used to serve others and bring glory to God. Recognize that challenges and uncertainties are part of the process, and they are opportunities for personal and spiritual growth.

Prompts for Journaling and Self-Reflection
Use the following prompts as a guide for your journaling and self-reflection. Writing down your thoughts and experiences can provide clarity, deepen your understanding, and inspire continued growth as a solution provider.
Overcoming Doubt and Fear: Recall a time when doubt and fear hindered your progress. How did you overcome these challenges, and what did you learn from the experience?

Practical Exercises and Reflection Questions to Help You Apply the Concepts
Exercise:
- ✓ Develop a mantra or affirmation to use when doubt or fear arises. Practice using this mantra in moments of uncertainty.

Reflection Questions:
- ✓ How did your chosen mantra help you overcome doubt or fear?
- ✓ What steps can you take to trust in God's plan during challenging times?

Action Plan with Strategies to Help You Take Forward and Implement

Action Plan: Develop a daily affirmation or mantra that reminds you to trust in God's plan during moments of doubt and fear. Repeat this affirmation as needed to re-center your faith.

Strategy: Draw inspiration from biblical stories of faith, such as Noah's obedience in building the ark despite doubt and ridicule. Analyze how their unwavering trust in God's plan led to remarkable outcomes.

As you immerse yourself in this chapter, reflect on the lesson of trusting in God's plan, drawing wisdom from Jeremiah 29:11, and the story of Gideon's faith. Develop an action plan that focuses on conquering fear and doubt through prayer, reflection, and seeking support. Embrace God's purpose for your life with unwavering faith, knowing that even in moments of doubt, His plan is one of hope, love, and a future filled with purpose.

Navigating Challenges and Overcoming Setbacks

In this journey of becoming a solution provider to the world, there's a reality we must confront—the inevitability of challenges and setbacks. Life is replete with obstacles, trials, and moments of adversity that test our resolve and determination. Yet, it's often in these very moments that our greatest opportunities for growth and personal development emerge. In this chapter, we delve into the profound lesson of resilience and growth through adversity, drawing wisdom from both biblical insights and real-world experiences. We'll explore the transformative power of challenges, examine the enduring endurance of biblical figures like Job, and equip you with practical strategies to develop resilience, maintain hope, and turn setbacks into stepping stones towards a brighter future. As we journey together through these pages, remember that setbacks are not roadblocks but opportunities to forge a stronger, more resilient path toward your purpose as a solution provider.

Lesson: Resilience and Growth through Adversity

Lesson Explanation: This chapter explores the vital lesson of resilience and personal growth that emerges from facing adversity.

Bible Verse: Romans 5:3-4

"We also glory in our sufferings, because we know that suffering produces perseverance; perseverance, character; and character, hope."

Verse Explanation: The selected Bible verse emphasizes the transformative power of adversity in shaping our character and fostering hope. It provides a strong foundation for understanding the value of resilience in the face of challenges.

Biblical Example: Job's Endurance
Biblical Example Explanation: Job's story is a timeless illustration of unwavering endurance and faith in the midst of immense suffering. His experience serves as an inspirational example of resilience through adversity.

Action Plan: Developing Resilience in the Face of Challenges
Action Plan Steps:
Self-Reflection: Encourage readers to reflect on past challenges and setbacks they've faced, considering the lessons learned and personal growth achieved.
Mindset Shift: Guide readers in shifting their mindset from viewing setbacks as failures to seeing them as opportunities for growth.
Resilience Building: Offer practical strategies for building resilience, such as cultivating a support network, practicing self-care, and developing problem-solving skills.
Goal Setting: Encourage readers to set realistic goals for overcoming challenges, emphasizing the importance of persistence.

Strategy: Turning Setbacks into Opportunities for Growth
Strategies for Implementation:

Positive Reframing: Teach readers how to reframe setbacks as opportunities for learning and personal development, fostering a more optimistic outlook.
Adaptive Coping: Provide coping strategies to help individuals navigate adversity effectively, such as stress management techniques and seeking support.
Goal Achievement: Offer guidance on setting SMART (Specific, Measurable, Achievable, Relevant, Time-bound) goals to ensure readers can track their progress in overcoming setbacks.

Prompts for Journaling and Self-Reflection

Journaling Prompts:

Reflect on a significant challenge you've faced in the past. How did you initially perceive it, and what lessons did you eventually derive from it?

Describe a time when adversity tested your resilience. How did you respond, and what personal growth emerged from that experience?

Practical Exercises and Reflection Questions to Help You Apply the Concepts

Practical Exercises:

- ✓ Create a "Resilience Toolbox" with strategies and resources you can turn to during challenging times.
- ✓ Write a letter to your future self, envisioning how you will overcome a current setback and the personal growth you will achieve in the process.

Reflection Questions:

- ✓ How do you typically react when facing adversity, and how might you shift your response to better align with resilience and personal growth?

- ✓ What steps can you take to build a support network that will help you navigate challenges effectively?

Action Plan with Strategies to Help You Take Forward and Implement

Action Plan Steps:

- ✓ Identify a current setback or challenge in your life that you can approach with resilience and a growth mindset.
- ✓ Apply the strategies discussed in this chapter, such as positive reframing and goal setting, to address the identified challenge.
- ✓ Monitor your progress and regularly reflect on the lessons learned and personal growth experienced throughout the process.

This chapter equips readers with valuable insights and practical tools to not only navigate challenges but also transform setbacks into opportunities for personal growth and resilience. It emphasizes the importance of maintaining hope and faith in the face of adversity, drawing inspiration from both biblical wisdom and real-world examples.

Examples of How Solution Providers Identify Opportunities

People who excel as solution providers possess the ability to identify opportunities and pursue them with purpose and determination. Here are examples, both biblical and worldly, illustrating how they identify and pursue opportunities:

1. Biblical Example: Joseph

Opportunity Identification: Joseph, in the book of Genesis, identified the opportunity to interpret Pharaoh's dreams, foreseeing a famine. He realized this could be an opportunity to save Egypt and neighboring lands from starvation.

Pursuit: Joseph not only interpreted the dreams but also proposed a comprehensive plan to store grain during the years of abundance. He actively pursued the opportunity to implement this plan and managed the food distribution during the famine, ultimately saving countless lives.

2. Worldly Example: Thomas Edison

Opportunity Identification: Thomas Edison identified the opportunity to improve upon existing electric lighting systems. He recognized the potential for creating a practical and commercially viable electric light.

Pursuit: Edison conducted extensive research and experimentation to develop the incandescent light bulb. He filed numerous patents related to electric lighting and went on to establish the Edison Electric Light Company, pioneering the widespread use of electric lighting.

3. Biblical Example: Esther

Opportunity Identification: Esther, in the Book of Esther, recognized an opportunity to use her position as queen to advocate for the Jewish people when they faced extermination.

Pursuit: She took the bold step of approaching King Xerxes to intercede on behalf of her people, putting her own life at risk. Her courage and timely action resulted in a decree that saved the Jewish community.

4. Worldly Example: Malala Yousafzai

Opportunity Identification: Malala Yousafzai identified the opportunity to advocate for girls' education and women's rights, particularly in regions where access to education was limited.

Pursuit: Despite facing threats and violence from the Taliban, Malala continued to speak out for education. She co-authored the memoir "I Am Malala," became a global advocate, and received the Nobel Peace Prize for her efforts.

5. Biblical Example: Moses

Opportunity Identification: Moses, in the Book of Exodus, identified the opportunity to lead the Israelites out of slavery in Egypt after encountering the burning bush and hearing God's call.

Pursuit: Moses embraced this opportunity, confronted Pharaoh, and led the Israelites on a challenging journey to freedom in the Promised Land, guided by his faith and determination.

6. Worldly Example: Elon Musk

Opportunity Identification: Elon Musk identified the opportunity to accelerate humanity's transition to sustainable energy and address climate change through electric vehicles and renewable energy technologies.

Pursuit: He co-founded companies like Tesla, SpaceX, and SolarCity, actively pursuing advancements in electric vehicles, space exploration, and solar energy, all with the aim of addressing pressing global challenges.

These examples highlight that solution providers keenly observe their surroundings, are open to new possibilities, and take proactive steps to address pressing issues or create innovative solutions. They often possess a strong sense of purpose and determination to make a positive impact on their communities and the world.

JESUS: the Greatest Problem Solver- Examples and Lessons from His Life

Jesus, the Ultimate Problem Solver

In the tapestry of human existence, Jesus emerges as the quintessential Problem Solver, not merely addressing the immediate challenges of life but delving into the very core of humanity's most profound dilemmas. At the heart of His mission lies the unparalleled resolution to the greatest predicament—the separation of humanity from God, the consequence of sin. Jesus, the Savior, stands as the eternal answer, providing not only deliverance from eternal damnation but also ushering in a life of abundance, both in this world and the one to come.

1. **Salvation and Deliverance:** The pinnacle of Jesus' problem-solving prowess rests in His role as the Redeemer. Through His sacrificial death and resurrection, Jesus orchestrated the ultimate solution to the predicament of sin, offering humanity salvation and deliverance. This divine act ensures that those who believe in Him are not only forgiven but also liberated from the shackles of sin's eternal consequences.

2. **A Life of Abundance:** Jesus not only rescued us from the perils of spiritual separation but also ushered in a life of abundance. His promise in John 10:10 echoes through the ages, declaring, "I have come that they may have life, and have it to the full." This abundance transcends mere material prosperity; it encompasses a richness of purpose, joy, and eternal significance that only He can bestow.

3. **Healing the Sick:** In addressing physical ailments, Jesus demonstrated His compassion and power. The

healing miracles recorded in the Gospels reveal a Savior who not only sees the afflictions of His people but intervenes with divine healing. In doing so, He teaches us the lesson of empathy and the tangible expression of love for those in need.

4. Feeding the Multitudes: The miraculous feeding of the 5,000 stands as a testament to Jesus' ability to address immediate, practical needs. By multiplying a few loaves and fish, He showcases divine resourcefulness and underscores the importance of trusting in God's provision for our daily sustenance.

5. Forgiving Sins: Beyond physical ailments, Jesus delved into the root cause of humanity's brokenness—sin. The forgiveness of sins, exemplified in instances like the paralytic lowered through the roof, illuminates the profound spiritual healing available through His redemptive work. This teaches us the lesson of the paramount significance of spiritual restoration.

6. Raising the Dead: In the raising of Lazarus and other instances, Jesus manifests His authority over death. Conquering humanity's greatest fear, He instills unwavering faith in His followers, assuring them of eternal life through Him.

7. Teaching and Guiding: Jesus, the preeminent Teacher, not only performed miracles but also provided timeless guidance for navigating life's complexities. His parables and teachings offer solutions to moral dilemmas, guiding us toward a life characterized by love, humility, and servanthood.

In every facet of His life, Jesus stands as the ultimate Problem Solver. From the eternal dilemma of sin to the daily challenges of existence, His transformative power continues to guide and inspire, beckoning us to follow His example of compassion, wisdom, and unwavering faith. Jesus, the greatest Problem Solver, extends an invitation to abundant life, both now and for all eternity.

Finally, The Ultimate Solution: Jesus Lives in Us

In a world filled with challenges and uncertainties, we are often in search of solutions. We seek answers to complex problems, yearning for a way to mend brokenness and find purpose. In this quest for answers, we discover that the ultimate solution has been with us all along—Jesus Christ. Through faith in Him, we not only find answers but carry the solution within us. This chapter delves into the profound truth that Jesus is the incomparable solution to humanity's deepest needs, offering forgiveness, redemption, and the promise of eternal life.

Lesson: The Incomparable Solution

In the chaos of our world, it's easy to lose sight of the uniqueness of Jesus as the ultimate solution. His life, teachings, and sacrifice stand apart as the answer to our most profound questions and concerns. Jesus is the embodiment of love, mercy, and grace. He offers forgiveness for our sins, redemption from our brokenness, and the promise of eternal life with Him. In Him, we find hope that transcends the challenges we face, and through Him, we experience transformation.

Bible Verse: John 14:6

"Jesus answered, 'I am the way and the truth and the life. No one comes to the Father except through me.'"

This verse is a profound reminder that Jesus is the exclusive path to God the Father. He is not merely a solution but the very essence of truth, life, and salvation. Through Jesus, we access a relationship with our Heavenly Father that offers unparalleled hope and purpose.

Biblical Example: The Apostle Paul

The life of the Apostle Paul provides a powerful illustration of how encountering Jesus can transform a person's entire existence. Paul, once a persecutor of Christians, had a life-changing encounter with Jesus on the road to Damascus. This encounter not only converted him to Christianity but also ignited a passionate devotion to spreading the Gospel. His unwavering faith in Jesus as the ultimate solution led him to endure hardship, persecution, and suffering for the sake of Christ.

Action Plan: Embracing Jesus as the Solution

- ✓ **Faith and Salvation:** Faith in Jesus is the gateway to salvation and eternal life. Through faith, we accept the forgiveness and redemption He offers.
- ✓ **Relationship with Christ:** Cultivate a personal relationship with Jesus through daily prayer, studying the Word of God, and engaging in heartfelt worship. This relationship is the cornerstone of our journey with Him.
- ✓ **Transformation:** Jesus not only forgives our sins but transforms us into His image. Embrace the process of personal transformation by surrendering to His will, allowing Him to mold your character and life.

Strategy: Carrying Jesus to the World

- ✓ **Witnessing and Evangelism:** We are called to share the Gospel and the hope found in Jesus with others. Develop strategies for effective witnessing and evangelism, always relying on the Holy Spirit for guidance.

- ✓ **Living as Salt and Light:** As believers, we are called to reflect the character of Christ in our daily lives. Be intentional about living as salt and light in your community, workplace, and interactions with others.
- ✓ **Service and Compassion:** Jesus's life was characterized by selfless service and compassion for the marginalized. Follow His example by seeking opportunities to serve others and demonstrate His love.

Prompts for Journaling and Self-Reflection

Take time to reflect on your personal relationship with Jesus. How has your faith in Him influenced your daily life, decisions, and interactions with others? Journal about specific moments when you've experienced Jesus as the ultimate solution to challenges or questions you've faced.

Practical Exercises and Reflection Questions to Help You Apply the Concepts

Exercise: Daily Devotional Time

Commit to establishing a daily devotional routine to deepen your connection with Jesus. Set aside dedicated time for prayer, Bible study, and reflection.

Exercise: Community Involvement

Seek ways to actively engage with your local community, demonstrating Christ's love through your actions. Consider volunteering, supporting local charities, or participating in community events.

Exercise: Missions and Outreach

Explore opportunities for mission work and outreach programs, whether locally or globally. Discover how you can impact lives and share the message of Jesus as the ultimate solution.

Action Plan with Strategies to Help You Take Forward and Implement

- ✓ **Daily Devotional Time:** Develop a personalized daily devotional routine that includes prayer, Scripture reading, and meditation on God's Word. This practice will deepen your relationship with Jesus.
- ✓ **Community Involvement:** Identify specific ways you can engage with your community, showing Christ's love through acts of kindness and service. Consider joining local outreach initiatives or starting one of your own.
- ✓ **Missions and Outreach:** Explore opportunities for mission trips, volunteering, or supporting organizations dedicated to spreading the Gospel and addressing social needs. Be intentional about carrying Jesus to the world.

In closing, we affirm the profound truth that Jesus is the ultimate solution to the world's greatest needs. Through faith in Him, we not only discover answers but carry the very presence of the Solution within us. We challenge you to embrace your role as a bearer of this life-changing truth. As carriers of Christ's love, forgiveness, and redemption, we have the privilege and responsibility to impact the world around us positively. Let us go forth, carrying Jesus in our hearts and sharing His transformative message with a world in need, for He is the Ultimate Solution, and He lives in us.

31 Declarations You can Use to Prophesy over Your Life Daily as You Embrace Your Role as a Solution Provider

Here's a list of 31 decrees and declarations along with relevant Bible verses that you can use to prophesy over your life daily as you embrace your role as a solution provider: Proclaiming these decrees daily, coupled with meditation on the corresponding Bible verses, can empower you to embrace your role as a solution provider and make a positive impact in the world.

Day 1: Decree of Purpose *Declaration:* I am created for a purpose, to be a solution provider in this world. *Bible Verse:* Jeremiah 1:5 - "Before I formed you in the womb I knew you, before you were born I set you apart..."
Day 2: Decree of Compassion *Declaration:* I have a heart full of compassion for others and their needs. *Bible Verse:* Colossians 3:12 - "Therefore, as God's chosen people, holy and dearly loved, clothe yourselves with compassion..."
Day 3: Decree of Wisdom *Declaration:* I seek divine wisdom to solve complex problems. *Bible Verse:* James 1:5 - "If any of you lacks wisdom, you should ask God, who gives generously to all without finding fault..."
Day 4: Decree of Integrity *Declaration:* I walk in honesty and integrity in all my dealings. *Bible Verse:*

Proverbs 11:3 - "The integrity of the upright guides them..."

Day 5: Decree of Resilience *Declaration:* I overcome obstacles with perseverance and resilience. *Bible Verse:* Philippians 4:13 - "I can do all things through him who gives me strength."

Day 6: Decree of Collaboration *Declaration:* I work harmoniously with others for a common goal. *Bible Verse:* Ecclesiastes 4:9 - "Two are better than one, because they have a good return for their labor."

Day 7: Decree of Generosity *Declaration:* I generously share my blessings to impact lives. *Bible Verse:* Luke 6:38 - "Give, and it will be given to you. A good measure, pressed down, shaken together and running over..."

Day 8: Decree of Impact *Declaration:* I am leaving a lasting legacy of positive impact. *Bible Verse:* Matthew 5:16 - "Let your light shine before others, that they may see your good deeds and glorify your Father in heaven."

Day 9: Decree of Humility *Declaration:* I remain grounded in humility despite achievements. *Bible Verse:* Proverbs 27:2 - "Let someone else praise you, and not your own mouth; an outsider, and not your own lips."

Day 10: Decree of Trust *Declaration:* I trust in God's plan for my life, knowing it's for good. *Bible Verse:* Jeremiah 29:11 - "For I know the plans I have for you, plans to prosper you and not to harm you, plans to give you hope and a future."

Day 11: Decree of Empathy *Declaration:* I cultivate a heart of empathy and understanding. *Bible Verse:* Romans 12:15 - "Rejoice with those who rejoice; mourn with those who mourn."

Day 12: Decree of Collaboration *Declaration:* I leverage collective strength to make a difference. *Bible Verse:* Romans 12:4-5 - "For just as each of us has one body with many members, and these members do not all have the same function, so in Christ we, though many, form one body, and each member belongs to all the others."

Day 13: Decree of Integrity *Declaration:* I am known for unwavering integrity in all I do. *Bible Verse:* Proverbs 10:9 - "Whoever walks in integrity walks securely..."

Day 14: Decree of Perseverance *Declaration:* I remain committed in the face of challenges. *Bible Verse:* Hebrews 10:36 - "You need to persevere so that when you have done the will of God, you will receive what he has promised."

Day 15: Decree of Vision *Declaration:* I have a clear vision to solve problems and create change. *Bible Verse:* Proverbs 29:18 - "Where there is no vision, the people perish..."

Day 16: Decree of Impact *Declaration:* I am a source of encouragement and support to others. *Bible Verse:* 1 Thessalonians 5:11 - "Therefore encourage one another and build each other up..."

Day 17: Decree of Humility *Declaration:* I remain humble in my achievements, giving glory to God. *Bible Verse:* James 4:10 - "Humble yourselves before the Lord, and he will lift you up."

Day 18: Decree of Trust *Declaration:* I trust in God's guidance for every decision I make. *Bible Verse:* Proverbs 3:5-6 - "Trust in the Lord with all your heart and lean not on your own understanding; in all your ways submit to him, and he will make your paths straight."

Day 19: Decree of Wisdom *Declaration:* I seek divine wisdom in every challenge I face. *Bible Verse:* Proverbs 2:6 - "For the Lord gives wisdom; from his mouth come knowledge and understanding."

Day 20: Decree of Resilience *Declaration:* I view setbacks as opportunities for growth. *Bible Verse:* Romans 8:28 - "And we know that in all things God works for the good of those who love him, who have been called according to his purpose."

Day 21: Decree of Compassion *Declaration:* I express compassion to those in need every day. *Bible Verse:* Ephesians 4:32 - "Be kind and compassionate to one another..."

Day 22: Decree of Generosity *Declaration:* I generously give of my time, resources, and love. *Bible Verse:* Acts 20:35 - "It is more blessed to give than to receive."

Day 23: Decree of Vision *Declaration:* I see opportunities where others see obstacles. *Bible Verse:* Isaiah 43:19 - "See, I am doing a new thing! Now it springs up; do you not perceive it?"

Day 24: Decree of Impact *Declaration:* I am leaving a legacy that will bless future generations. *Bible Verse:* Psalm 145:4 - "One generation commends your works to another; they tell of your mighty acts."

Day 25: Decree of Collaboration *Declaration:* I work in harmony with others to achieve great things. *Bible Verse:* Psalm 133:1 - "How good and pleasant it is when God's people live together in unity!"

Day 26: Decree of Trust *Declaration:* I trust God's timing for every aspect of my journey. *Bible Verse:* Ecclesiastes 3:1 - "There is a time for everything, and a season for every activity under the heavens."

Day 27: Decree of Integrity *Declaration:* I am a person of unwavering integrity in all circumstances.

Bible Verse: Psalm 25:21 - "May integrity and uprightness protect me, because my hope, Lord, is in you."

Day 28: Decree of Perseverance *Declaration:* I persist in the face of challenges, knowing that victory is near. *Bible Verse:* Galatians 6:9 - "Let us not become weary in doing good, for at the proper time we will reap a harvest if we do not give up."

Day 29: Decree of Humility *Declaration:* I remain humble, acknowledging that all talents are gifts from God. *Bible Verse:* 1 Peter 5:6 - "Humble yourselves, therefore, under God's mighty hand, that he may lift you up in due time."

Day 30: Decree of Wisdom *Declaration:* I seek divine wisdom to make informed decisions. *Bible Verse:* Proverbs 4:7 - "Wisdom is the principal thing; therefore get wisdom..."

Day 31: Decree of Impact *Declaration:* I am a solution provider to the world, impacting lives for God's glory. *Bible Verse:* Matthew 5:13-14 - "You are the salt of the earth... You are the light of the world."

Reflecting on the Lessons

As we draw this journey of becoming a solution provider to a close, it's important to reflect on the profound lessons we've explored and the transformative impact they can have on our lives and the lives of those we touch.

Embracing Your Role as a Solution Provider We have discovered that each one of us is uniquely crafted with gifts and talents, a purposeful creation of the Divine. Recognizing and embracing our roles as solution providers is not only a privilege but a sacred duty. Our journey is guided by the principle that we are here to serve others, to be the hands and feet of God in a world filled with challenges.

Continuously Growing in Your Calling Our journey as solution providers is not static but dynamic, characterized by continuous growth and self-improvement. Just as a tree grows and bears fruit, we too must nurture our gifts and talents, cultivating them to their fullest potential. Through prayer, reflection, and the wisdom of the Scriptures, we can refine our abilities, sharpen our skills, and deepen our impact.

Leaving a Legacy of Impact Finally, we have explored the concept of legacy—a legacy of impact that endures beyond our lifetime. In this concluding chapter, we have seen that our legacy is not merely about the tangible achievements or possessions we leave behind, but the enduring mark we make in the lives of others. It is about the love, kindness, and positive change we sow in the world, creating a ripple effect that touches future generations.

In this journey, we have drawn inspiration from the Scriptures, taking solace in verses such as Jeremiah 29:11, Proverbs 27:2, and Matthew 5:16. We have found strength and guidance in the lives of biblical figures like Esther, Gideon, and King David, who exemplified the lessons we've explored.

As we reflect on the profound lessons we've explored throughout this journey, let us firmly grasp the truth that Jesus is the ultimate solution, and His presence lives within us. We are not just seekers of answers; we are walking answers to the world, carrying His transformative message wherever we go.

To conclude, let us remember that being a solution provider is not a solitary endeavor but a shared calling that unites us in purpose. As we continue on this path, may we find courage in the face of doubt, compassion in our interactions with others, wisdom in our decision-making, integrity in our actions, and humility in our successes. Let us leave a legacy of love, hope, and positive change, knowing that our calling as solution providers is a sacred mission with the power to transform the world, one act of service at a time.

Conclusion

As we reach the final chapter of this journey, I want you to take a moment to reflect on the path we've traveled together. It's been a journey of self-discovery, of uncovering your unique purpose, and of understanding the profound impact you can have on the world as a solution provider.

Throughout these pages, we've delved into the lessons of empathy, wisdom, integrity, perseverance, and humility, all guided by the timeless wisdom of the Scriptures. We've walked alongside biblical figures who exemplified these virtues, drawing inspiration from their stories and experiences.

But this journey is not just about knowledge; it's about transformation. It's about taking what we've learned and putting it into action. It's about becoming the solution provider you were meant to be.

Remember, your purpose is not a mere concept—it's a living, breathing reality waiting to be lived. You are here to make a difference, to bring light to the darkest corners, and to offer hope where it's needed most. Your unique gifts and talents are not accidents; they are your tools for change.

As you close this book, my hope is that you carry with you the profound lessons of compassion, wisdom, integrity, resilience, and humility. May you, like Esther, find the courage to stand up for what's right. May you, like Gideon, have unwavering faith in the face of doubt. May you, like King David, remain humble in your successes, and like Barnabas, may you always have a generous heart.

In your journey as a solution provider, may you continually seek divine guidance, trust in God's plan, and leave a legacy of impact that reverberates through generations. And as you do, remember that you are not alone; you are part of a tapestry of individuals working together to make the world a better place.

As we conclude this journey, let us remember that Jesus is the ultimate solution, and His presence lives within us. We are not just seekers of answers; we are walking answers to the world, carrying His transformative message wherever we go.

Thank you for taking this journey with me. The world is brighter because of your presence and the light you bring. Your purpose is not just a calling; it's a gift—a gift you share with the world.

About the Author 'GERARD ASSEY'

Gerard Assey is a Graduate in Economics, a PGD in Management (HRD) and holds a Doctorate in Leadership. Gerard holds several International Qualifications in Sales, Debt Collection, Training & Teaching, and is a 'Fellow' of the prestigious 'Institute of Sales & Marketing Management'-UK, a Certified NLP Practitioner, a 'Certified Trainer', an 'Accredited Management Teacher-Behavioral Sciences', a 'Certified Competency Facilitator', a 'Certified Management Consultant'- (the International credentials of a professional management consultant, awarded in accordance with global standards of the ICMCI); and a Certification from the University of Michigan in 'Successful Negotiation: Essential Strategies and Skills'

He is also a Member of the 'National Association of Sales Professionals' backed with several years experience in varied industries, both in India and Overseas. He also holds an 'Etiquette Consultant' Certification from the USA (by Sue Fox, Author of Best Seller: 'Business Etiquette for Dummies'. She has trained some of the top celebrities' world over). He was also a recipient of a scholarship for extensive training in Japan on 'Corporate Management for India'.

Gerard Assey is 'Founder & Chief Corporate Trainer' of the Group: '**Citius, Altius, Fortius Unlimited'**- an organization that **celebrated 20 years of Glorious Service** in 2021, focusing on 3 Core Competencies:

People. Performance. Profit; in functional areas of Sales & Marketing, HR & Organizational Development, covering Recruitment, Training & Consultancy!

Having managed organizations with large Sales Forces in India & Overseas, his specialization cover extensive areas of Sales Training (All levels - Presentation, Negotiation, Key/ Strategic Accounts Management & Managerial Skills for all sectors), Bid Proposal/ Capture Planning/ Management Trainings, Retail Sales, Customer Service & Customer Retention Programs, Training for Prevention & Collection of Debt, Self & Personal Development Programs (Time Management, Teamwork & Team Building, Business Etiquette & Personal Grooming, Leadership & Managerial Skills, People Management Skills, Train-the-Trainer etc), including preparation of Custom-designed Business Manuals for Internal (HR, Induction, and Sales etc) & External use (Instruction, User Manuals).

Gerard has successfully conducted over 6000 Trainings & Workshops (as of Oct '23) all across India, Middle East, Africa, Europe & S.E. Asia. Besides public programs conducted regularly, both in India & Overseas, he has some of the top names as clients whom he services from Single Owners to large Public & Government undertakings, covering all sectors, for their in-house needs.

His website: www.CollectionSkills.com is the only one in this part of the world to be featured in the 'Collections & Credit Risk Magazine-USA' under 'Who's Who in Training' and ranks TOP, along with other websites listed below on most search engines.

Gerard is author of 90 books already (Nov 2023),

A Few of the Business related Books being:

1. Bite-sized Bits on Commonsense Management
2. Heart to Heart on Life's Principles'
3. How to become a Successful Manager
4. The Sales Professionals' Master Workbook of S.Y.S.T.E.M.S
5. The Professional Business Email Etiquette Handbook & Guide
6. The Professional Business Video-Conferencing Etiquette Handbook & Guide
7. Professional Presentation Skills
8. Exceptional Customer Service
9. Professional Tele-Marketing Skills
10. Professional Debt Collection Skills
11. The G.R.E.A.T. Sales & Service Workbook
12. Sales Training Advantage for Results (*The Ultimate Sales Training Manual to enable you stand out as a S.T.A.R.*)
13. CEO Daily Planner & Organizer
14. The Sales Professionals' Master Daily Planner
15. The Professional Debt Collector's Master Daily Planner
16. My Daily Planner & Organizer
17. MY EMERGENCY INFORMATION RECORD (Family Emergency & Peace of Mind Planner)
18. The Ultimate Therapist & Counselors Planner and Organizer
19. Building an Ethical Workplace
20. Managing Relationships at Work
21. Managing Business Meetings Effectively
22. Effective Delegation Skills
23. Goal Setting for Success
24. B2B Selling by Email
25. Professional Business Etiquette & Grooming
26. Dining Etiquette & Table Manners
27. Effective Networking Skills
28. Grooming, Etiquette & Manners for Teens, Young Adults & Future Leaders
29. Inter-Personal Skills

30. Get Ready, Get Hired!
31. Selling in a Recession
32. Effective Receivables Management in an Economic Downturn!
33. Real Estate & Property Sales Training
34. Credit Sales & Accounts Receivable Management
35. Selling Skills for Real Estate & Property Advisors
36. Take G.R.E.A.T. C.A.R.E!
37. Spa, Salon & Health Club Selling Skills
38. Selling Travel, Holiday & MICE Services
39. Selling Skills for Spa's, Salons & Health Clubs
40. Retailing in Salons & Spas
41. Selling Holiday, Vacation, Tours & Packages
42. The Power of Sales Referrals
43. Selling Luxury
44. Technical Selling Skills Financial Advisors Sales Training
45. Dealing with Burnout at Work
46. Monopolize Your Markets
47. Selling to Affluent Customers
48. Growing up with Grace
49. Financial Selling Skills
50. *The Effective Manager's Guide: Key Skills to Thrive*
51. From Aspiring to Inspiring: A Guide for New Managers on the Rise
52. The Power of Focus
53. Selling with Integrity: Sell Like Jesus The Perfect Role Model!
54. 31 Habits of Champions: Your 31-Day Journey to Greatness
55. Navigate the AI-Powered Future of Bid & Proposals: Up-Skill to Stay Relevant with Alternative Career Paths & Opportunities
56. Hiring Sales Winners
57. Present with Impact
58. Success Unlocked: *Breaking Free from Habits that Hold You Back*

59. Complaints to Cheers, Feedback to Gold: Mastering Complaints Management
60. Thriving Together: *Cultivating Diversity, Equity, and Inclusion*
61. Coaching Skills for Sales Managers
62. Soaring to Success in Business & Leadership: Swifter, Higher, Stronger!

...And some of his most recent Christian Books being:

1. A Bouquet of Praises for My KING
2. Christian Jokes for the Serious Religious' Folks!
3. Jesus Healed You!
4. Praise24Ever! (also in Tamil version)
5. The 5G Network of GOD
6. Building Faith over F.E.A.R- FACE EVERYTHING AND RISE with JESUS
7. Hebrew and Greek Praise and Worship Words
8. Godly Mothers' and Grandmothers' Bible Story time for Kids!
9. Miracles of Jesus in Pictures
10. Raise your Praise all 365 Days
11. Thanking GOD with an Attitude of Gratitude
12. Meditating on the Attributes of GOD
13. Puppet Scripts
14. Alcohol Ruins, JESUS Reforms, Renews & Restores!
15. Habakkuk 2:2 Christian Daily Journal, Planner & Organizer
16. ABC of GOD's Word for Handwriting Practice
17. Daily Bible Verse Handwriting Practice (Building Godly Character & Faith through Cursive Handwriting Practice!)
18. Guiding Light: Fun & Faith-Building Bible Activities for Children
19. Rejecting Grasshopper Talk: From Grasshopper to Giant-Killer-*Defeating Giants Daily!*
20. Teen Titans of Faith: *Building Courage,*

Determination & Christ-like-Esteem

21. I AM Empowered: *Unleashing Divine Power with Positive Declarations*
22. Be A Solution Provider-*From Passion to Purpose*: *A Biblical Guide to Being the Answer to the World!*

Besides regularly contributing to business & trade journals, including international ones such as the 'Creative Training Techniques' and the 'Sales News' of the U.S.A, He is also a member of several prestigious bodies & trade associations, having participated in many Conferences & Workshops in India & Overseas.

Prior to his last assignment of leading & managing a large MNC as head, Gerard had a 3-year stint in the Middle East as a Consultant with a leading British Consultancy Firm.

As the past 'Official Country Representative' for the International Business Award- 'THE STEVIES'-(the business world's own Oscar) for about 4 years- he ensured a few Indian companies that qualify for the same every year!

Gerard can be contacted at:
Email: training@Sales-Training.in,training@CollectionSkills.com
Websites:

www.Sales-Training.in
www.EtiquetteWorks.in
www.CollectionSkills.com
www.RetailSalesTraining.in
www.SalesTrainingIndia.com
www.ManualPreparation.com
www.TrainingWithPuppets.com
www.FirstContactAcademy.com
www.SalesAndMarketingRecruiter.com

Our TRAININGS & BOOKS that can help your team

- ✓ **Sales Effectiveness**: Selling Skills for any Sector: Service/ Logistics/ FMCG Realty/ Insurance & Finance/ Media/ SPA's, Health Clubs & Salons/ Key Account Management, Effective Negotiation Skills/ Bid & Proposal Management Skills/ Retail Sales Training: Any Sector (Auto, Jewelry, Clothing, Luxury etc)
- ✓ **Customer Service Skills**-Complaints Handling & Customer Retention
- ✓ **Debt Prevention & Collection Skills**
- ✓ **Etiquette & Grooming**
- ✓ **Leadership & Managerial Skills**
- ✓ **Self & Personal Development Skills**: Presentation Skills/ Effective Communication Skills/Business Proposal Writing Skills/ Problem Solving & Decision Making Skills/ Empowering Secretaries-The perfect PA! (For Secretaries & PA's)/ Effective Time Management/ Teamwork & Teambuilding/ P.R.I.D.E- **P**ersonal **R**esponsibility **I**n **D**elivering **E**xcellence

www.ingramcontent.com/pod-product-compliance
Lightning Source LLC
LaVergne TN
LVHW052030170826
845678LV00018B/2490

* 9 7 8 8 1 9 6 5 8 0 7 1 1 *